Kate H

How to Get Top Marks in …

Managing Poor Work Performance

The HR Headmistress' Guide

Other books by the same author:
Off the Sick List! How to Turn Employee Absence into Attendance

Praise for How to Get Top Marks in ...
Managing Poor Work Performance

A clear, no-nonsense, practical guide to managing poor performance in the workplace. It's straight-talking, comprehensive, yet easy to dip into, with some really useful checklists. A must-have desk companion for any self-assured HR professional.

Jo Mildren, HR Advisor, Impellam Support Services

The prospect of managing poor performance can be a scary process made worse by a complex legal framework. Written in a format that is easy to read, this guide provides practical information and advice that will help guide any manager through this difficult process. It is highly recommended for both experienced and new managers.

Julie Mimnagh, Head of HR Operations, Enfield Council

Having spent years advising on performance management, it always sounded so simple until I was the one having to do it. This book provides a realistic viewpoint of just how difficult it is whilst guiding the user through the process in a practical way. Suddenly performance management is simple again and I've got a great tool to refer managers to.

Louise Campbell, Senior HR Officer, Childbase

A concise, punchy summary of the real issues faced in managing performance, with practical tips on how to resolve them. The 'learning from real life' examples made me smile, and sometimes squirm, and were great illustrations of how the legal requirements fit with day-to-day problems. The example checklists and letters are a valuable take-away.

Sue Almond, Director of Quality and Professional Standards, Kreston International

This book successfully demystifies the issue of improving work performance, and I liked the personal experiences, case studies and practical tips, which embellish the text.

John Stamford, John Stamford Associates, Companion CIPD

Concise and straightforward, it's the perfect guide for the HR practitioner to supplement the heavier reads and the ACAS code; particularly useful when in the smaller organisation advising managers through poor performance issues isn't necessarily a frequent or a formal occurrence.

The examples, checklists, and 'HR Headmistress tips' enable an easy yet informative read for managers too – I will certainly be circulating a copy!
Rachel Haime, Operations Manager, State of Flux Limited

Great read! A clear, common sense reference book for HR and Line Managers. The HR Headmistress provides comprehensive step-by-step support with clear working examples to facilitate effective, legally compliant, performance management. I look forward to reading other works from The HR Headmistress!
Kirsten McCartney
Controller, Human Resources, Nissan Technical Centre Europe

Refreshingly jargon free and practical. I came to this booklet seeking guidance on what constitutes sufficient support and development before taking action to dismiss. I found sound, no-nonsense, practical ideas described pithily and with clarity. Helpful distinctions are drawn between misconduct and lack of capability and the author takes a holistic view of the impact of poor performance both on other individuals and the organisation. The 'Learning from life's lessons' punctuate the text effectively and offer reality to the theory and legislation. I've thoroughly enjoyed reading it.
Christina Lloyd, Head of Teaching and Learner Support, Student Services,
The Open University

At a time when many employers are looking to get the best out of their employees, Kate Russell's latest book is a timely arrival. Contrary to popular belief, employment law has not taken away the "right to manage" and Kate's robust and practical approach to the topic is refreshing. Written in a practical, no-nonsense style, with tips and checklists throughout, this publication should prove an excellent guide for any manager or small business owner who needs to tackle under performance.
Derek Eccleston, Author of The Manager's Guide to Discipline

This book is a clear articulation of good practice with easily accessible practical tips, which demystify the whole process. The legal background in this difficult area is clearly presented. The focus on bringing about performance improvement is helpful. It will assist in building managers' confidence in tackling issues of performance - so vital for organisational success.

Sue Jennings, ACO - Business and Organisational Development,
Bedfordshire Probation Trust

This book is a great introduction and guide to managing poor work performance for both students and managers alike. The processes are logically written in a clear and straightforward manner with relevant real life examples. The tips and suggested structures (appendices) are a great basis for implementing the performance management processes into a business.

Sarah Hull, BA Human Resource Management student

I have recently had three conversations with business owners who have had very trying times with their relationships with their staff. Simply put, if they had had the opportunity to have read Kate's book it would have saved all a lot of grief and heartache – a must for anyone who is serious about managing performance.

Peter Roper, Speaker, MD Positive Ground, bestselling author and
President of the Professional Speaking Association

All too often businesses fail to realise their potential because managers do not identify and tackle under-performing staff earlier enough. With the emphasis on prevention rather than cure, The HR Headmistress provides real life examples, tips and checklists, in a handy, practical and top of the form guide, which even the busiest manager could apply.

Peter Taylor, Managing Director, John Laing Partnership Limited

Kate Russell's book on dealing with poor work performance provides a practical, street-wise approach to dealing with a topic that so many employers find troublesome. Drawing on a number of real life cases, Kate provides clear and sensible advice on dealing with a number of knotty issues making this book an invaluable aid for any employer.

Robert Haysom, Director, Haysom Silverton & Partners Ltd

This easy to read book provides a clear step-by-step guide and practical examples to equip line managers with the confidence to manage poor work performance. It gives useful advice on the questions to ask and areas to explore when seeking to improve performance.

Janet Pearson, Human Resources Manager, Institute of Legal Executives (ILEX) Group

This easy-to-read book is a fantastic manager's guide for managing work performance. It provides experience from an author, 'The HR Headmistress', which includes her vast experience of working with organisations. The 'Learning from life's lessons' are a real hit. Practical checklists and sample documents make this a must-read for all managers who would like to have that 'difficult conversation' with their staff.

Simon Errington, People & Organisational Development Manager, North Yorkshire Fire & Rescue Service

How to Get Top Marks in ... Managing Poor Work Performance is packed with good practical advice for anyone having to deal with HR issues in the workplace. It is easy to read and gives plenty of real situations, which any employer will find familiar. More than that, it helps you in dealing with or avoiding those tricky situations that, if not handled right, can be so time consuming and expensive for a director or business owner. Essential reading for any manager.

Jonathan Bailey, Chairman, IoD, Milton Keynes

Kate Russell is a no-nonsense 'HR Headmistress'! She gives managers new and old an easy-to-access resource on how to manage poor performance. This must be the least favourite job any manager has to undertake but with Kate's clearly illustrated 'Learning from life's lessons', checklists, and her own HR Headmistress tips, managers cannow turn staff around and lead highly effective teams. I enjoyed it immensely. I liked the easy read with no waffle approach. It is directed at managers managing poor performance not HR managers helping managers manage poor performance – perfect for the modern day organisation. I will certainly be recommending it to colleagues and friends alike.

Rose-Marie Usher, IFR Manager, NHS Northamptonshire

A good read, informative and interesting. The HR Headmistress tips were also a nice touch to the book. This is perfect for anyone who has to deal with poor work performance. Kate Russell has succeeded in combining an explanation of what poor work performance is and how it is defined legally with her own experience within the area, and has created a tool kit to help solve those delicate, hard to approach problems with work performance.

Ace Bradburn, third year student BA Management

Easy to read, simple to understand and a brilliantly written guide that gets straight to the point. I am sure that after you read this book the complex and often mysterious world of employment law is no longer so. I recommend every manager or director (HR or not) keeps a copy on their desk because one thing they can be sure of is that sooner or later they will need to use it.

Hamid Khajehpour, IT & Logistics Consultant

During difficult economic climates, ensuring that employees are fulfilling their side of the employment contract is essential. Kate Russell's book on managing work performance contains practical advice and templates for managers and an explanation of the legal framework. There are useful tips to help employers do things fairly and it's an invaluable guide for preventing and solving performance issues.

G. Eddy, HR, Hawkins & Associates Ltd.

As an occupational health provider we are often asked to provide independent medical opinion on an individual's ability to perform their job function. In many, many cases the employer has "medicalised" what is essentially a management issue. Managing Poor Work Performance is a highly effective, easy to follow and essential business tool.

Matthew Kelvie, Commercial Director, Health Assured Ltd

About the author

After studying for a degree in business law, Kate Russell qualified as a barrister. She gained several years experience in operations, moved into human resources and later became a training specialist working in the manufacturing, distribution and service sectors.

She started Russell HR Consulting in 1998 and now divides her time between advising businesses of all sizes on HR issues and delivering a range of highly practical employment law awareness training to line managers, including a range of public workshops. Her unique combination of legal background, direct line management experience and HR skills enables Kate to present the stringent requirements of the law balanced against the realities of working life. She is a senior presenter for several companies and a popular public speaker. Kate completed an MA in strategic human resource management in 2004.

Kate is known as The HR Headmistress due to her combination of a devastating ability to cut through the mire, a certain briskness and unwillingness to tolerate absurdities and steely gaze over the reading glasses, all of which tend to make some people quiver. After a while, she stopped trying to pretend to be soft and fluffy and embraced her headmistress persona wholeheartedly. Well, 'if life hands you a lemon, make lemonade and sell it!'

She is the author of several practical employment handbooks and e-books, the highly acclaimed audio update service *Law on the Move*, as well as a monthly e-newsletter, the latter document neatly combining the useful, topical and the frivolous.

For more information about Russell HR Consulting, visit www.russellhrconsulting.co.uk

Acknowledgements

Writing the book is the (relatively) easy bit ... the process of getting the manuscript to book form is much harder! My thanks therefore go to:

My lovely team, especially Darry Khajehpour who's done so much of the legwork in helping me to create the book, has had some brilliant ideas along the way and has been such a support. In particular he was a star on the day we sweltered over printers producing the manuscripts for pre-publication review on the hottest day of the year. It was a Tennessee Williams ('It's so hot, Big Daddy!') meets national union of print workers (unrepeatable!) moment; Helen Cottrell who has offered ideas, tea (I run on tea) and a gentle belief in me – even when the book was just a twinkle in my laptop's eye, which was for a lo-o-o-ong time; my good friend and colleague Andrea Hughes who tells me I must mention her a) because she sent me some research material and b) because she kept things running smoothly when I was up to my ears in ink. I am delighted to acknowledge her contribution, the cheeky wench!

All those who helped to create the finished product; Helen Coolen, our efficient and encouraging editor; Caroline Massingham who has designed another great cover and is always so helpful even when we dither a bit; Suzie Tatnell of Commercial Campaigns for helping create the 'look' and steering us through the technical process from book block to publishing; and Robert Spicer who undertook the painstaking task of indexing.

Maria 'fab shoes' Kennedy of cremePR for helping to promote the book and MyTechie's Jude Hanlon (mother of the cucumber fiend) for making me laugh and creating the website.

All the pre-publication reviewers who have said such lovely things about the book, especially my 'favourite uncle' and wily employment tribunal expert John Stamford, who pointed out improvements to refine the text.

Last but not least, thanks as ever to Peter for not only putting up with all my crazy ideas, but taking them seriously and helping me bring them to life.

You're all brilliant!

Contents

Appendices

Contents

Miscellaneous notes

Statutory limits
Today's statutory limits have not been specified in this book as they go out of date so quickly. You can email info@russellhrconsulting.co.uk for an up-to-date copy of statutory limits.

Keep up-to-date with employment law
Sign up for Kate's free e-newsletter:
subscribe@russellhrconsulting.co.uk

Disclaimer
Whilst every effort has been made to ensure that the contents of the book are accurate and up to date, no responsibility will be accepted for any inaccuracies found.

This book should not be taken as a definitive guide or as a stand-alone document on all aspects of employment law. You should therefore seek legal advice where appropriate. The procedures referred to here are for guidance and you should follow their own procedure as authority levels and the number of steps in your procedure may differ from those set out in the book.

The material produced here is the property of Kate Russell and may not be reproduced without permission.

Gender description
For convenience and brevity I have referred to 'he' and 'him' throughout the book. It is intended to refer to both male and female employees.

Abbreviations

ACAS	Advice, Conciliation and Arbitration Service
CA	Court of Appeal
CIPD	Chartered Institute of Personnel & Development
DDA	Disability Discrimination Act 1995
DWP	Department of Work and Pensions
EAT	Employment Appeal Tribunal
ECHR	European Court of Human Rights
ECJ	European Court of Justice
EEA	European Economic Area
ERA	Employment Rights Act 1996
HMRC	Her Majesty's Revenue and Customs
HSE	Health and Safety Executive
LEL	Lower earnings limit
PIP	Performance improvement plan
SOSR	Some other substantial reason
SSP	Statutory Sick Pay
WTR	Working Time Regulations 1998

Introduction

The aim of How to Get Top Marks in ... Managing Poor Work Performance is to explain the legal framework, discuss the process of managing poor work performance effectively and to offer practical guidance, hints, tips, and HR Headmistress tactics (it's all about tactics).

This is not an academic treatise. There are no models, theories and writing in the passive tense here. It is essentially a tool kit for sorting out a problem, complete with checklists, templates and suggestions to make life a bit easier for you. Examples have been included to help illustrate the points made. Where I have drawn on cases from my own experience, names and some other details have been changed to protect the identities of the individuals.

I will be talking straight to you in exactly the same way as I would write an email to a client who is asking for advice. I shall be using everyday English, saying 'you' and generally writing as I would speak.

Employment law can be fun and I hope you find it useful.

Enjoy the book.

Capability:
what this book does
not cover

The Employment Rights Act 1996 (ERA) sets out the various fair reasons for dismissal. One of them is capability, or more precisely, a lack of capability. For the purposes of this book, poor performance and a lack of capability may be referred to variously as 'poor work performance', 'capability', 'competence' or 'incompetence', depending on the context.

Readers should note that under the ERA, capability has two other meanings; these are lack of capability on grounds of ill health or failure to acquire, or loss of, an essential qualification.

Performance reviews are often confused with managing poor work performance; performance review is another way of saying performance appraisal. Although a performance appraisal will formally review an employee's performance against specified targets and result in the giving and receiving of feedback, it should be an exchange and consolidation of information that is already known to both parties. You can refer to ongoing disciplinary issues during a performance appraisal, but it should never result in a disciplinary sanction.

This book deals purely with managing poor work performance. It does not deal with ill health, qualifications or performance appraisal.

The business need to manage poor work performance

Poor work performance is a subject of complaint raised far more often than misconduct. It's far less well addressed too, for all sorts of reasons.

Sometimes a manager feels rather unkind giving what he perceives as a 'telling off' to a nice, well-meaning employee who is not competent. The manager might be very busy and somehow that chat about poor performance never makes it to the top of his to-do list. Other managers fear confrontation; these days it is quite common for a manager who is giving guidance and correction for poor work performance to become the subject of a grievance, often citing bullying, harassment and victimisation. All of that makes work life incredibly stressful for managers.

HR Headmistress tip

Make sure your dignity at work procedure includes a phrase that says something like this:

'Note that managers have a right and duty to manage. A distinction must be made between the type of conduct described above (examples of genuine bullying and harassment) and a manager asking and encouraging an employee to carry out his duties to the required company standards. As part of the process, a manager will be required to monitor an employee's progress and give feedback on a regular basis. This is entirely normal. It is designed to support the employee and does not constitute bullying, harassment or victimisation.'

Being a manager means getting work done through your team. It can be tough. One thing you should remember is that you're not carrying out a manager's role to be best buddies with your employees. You're there to do a job fairly, lawfully, ethically and efficiently. If you can establish friendly relationships along the way, so much the better, but to perform the managerial role well, you need a degree of separation from your employees.

Putting off dealing with employees who are not delivering what you need is the worst thing to do. In the short term it might be easier to work round a poor performer, but quite quickly, other employees get fed up with carrying a colleague and grumble about covering for him. If you don't manage poor performance it can cause resentment and impact negatively on those employees who are performing satisfactorily, resulting in decreased workforce productivity (a team works at the pace of the slowest member). In severe cases, poor performance could lead to an increase of workplace accidents. Alternatively, you could end up doing the work, or it may be that the work just doesn't get done. Either way, it's not satisfactory.

Managing poor work performance should be part of an overall performance-management process, which also includes carrying out regular appraisals as well as identifying and meeting learning and development needs.

HR Headmistress tip

When giving feedback, balance is important. Remember to give praise for good work where it's due.

The benefits of managing competence effectively are fairly obvious:

- ✓ increased financial returns, e.g. profit after tax, earnings per share, market share
- ✓ increased productivity, decreased wastage
- ✓ reduced staff turnover and levels of absence
- ✓ improved feedback from employee or customer surveys
- ✓ less quantifiable but equally important information, such as staff satisfaction and staff development.

In difficult economic times, it's important to ensure that we achieve optimum performance from our employees.

About poor work performance

'Capability' refers to an employee's skills, ability, aptitude and knowledge in relation to the job that he is employed to do. Lack of capability is not the employee's fault and few employees choose to carry out their work badly, make mistakes, fail to complete tasks, or have poor relationships with colleagues or customers.

Learning from life's lessons

A client came to me and said that Gerry, an employee who had been with his company for some time, was unable to properly carry out his duties and was causing serious productivity problems. The employer wanted to know if he could sack Gerry, expressed his considerable frustration and said 'He's always been like this; slow to learn and loses the skills he does manage to gain quickly'.

He paused long enough in the diatribe to allow me to ask how long Gerry had been working there. I expected the employer to say something like, 'About six months.' I was amazed when the reply was '15 years – and he's always been useless…'

The example above is an extreme case, but the circumstances are common; we call it the ostrich manoeuvre in our office. Doing nothing will get you nowhere and as well as annoying you, it usually demotivates other, more competent employees.

Do note that there is a distinction to be made between incapability and misconduct. In simple terms you can define incapability as 'can't meet your standards' and misconduct as 'won't meet your standards'.

A lack of capability exists where the employee is unable to carry out the job to the standard required by the employer, even if he is genuinely trying to do so. It is the company's standard that is relevant, and not the manager's personal opinion of the employee.

If an employee fails to come up to the required standard as a result of his carelessness, negligence or idleness, this will not constitute lack of capability, but misconduct.

Often, a lack of capability will be outside the employee's direct control. For example, it would be unrealistic to blame an employee for poor work performance where the root cause of the problem is that adequate training has not been provided; that would be a capability matter. Generally, an employee will have control over his conduct at work. If an employee fails to make the necessary effort to do his job, that's a conduct matter.

It can sometimes be difficult to determine whether an employee's poor performance is due to inherent incapability or whether it is laziness, negligence or a lack of effort. In some cases, there may be an element of all of these factors. In the first instance, give the employee the benefit of the doubt and performance manage the employee informally.

Where you have a poor work performance issue, try to identify the cause of the problem. Busy managers might be tempted to assume that performance problems arise because of an employee's carelessness or lack of effort; some employees will be guilty of this, but don't assume it. There are a number of possible causes of poor performance. The cause of the poor work performance should emerge when you carry out an investigation.

Learning from life's lessons

An employer found a series of mistakes in work produced by a woman who assembled small electronic components. It was close work and required meticulous attention to detail. We tested her knowledge (it was fine) and she was very diligent and careful.

We were mystified until during the investigation we asked a question which made us realise that she needed spectacles for close work. Once she'd been provided with these, the mistakes stopped.

The first step is to investigate the cause of the unsatisfactory performance with the employee, the solution to the problem should then become apparent. If you can remove or reduce the cause of the problem, the employee's performance is likely to improve.

Let's start by finding out about the legal rights and responsibilities of employers.

The legal framework

Although this book is about getting the practical steps right, rather than quoting lots of employment law, you do need to know that the Employment Rights Act 1996 (ERA) sets out fair reasons for dismissal. Capability is one of the potentially fair reasons for dismissal, provided of course that you have properly followed your procedure and demonstrated that you have been fair. Dismissal is the last resort, but, carried out properly, it is fair.

Capability is defined in the Employment Rights Act 1996. Section 98 states that *'... capability, in relation to an employee, means his capability assessed by reference to skill, aptitude, health or any other physical or mental quality.'*

That's the law and clearly it's open to interpretation. For guidance on managing poor work performance on a day-to-day basis, we have to turn to the courts. They can be very useful for helping us determine the correct approach.

At various times the courts have concluded that someone who is a very slow worker, an inflexible worker who could not adapt, someone who fails to meet the employer's standards (even though the

Learning from life's lessons

St Leonard's School is an independent school. It has higher standards than those of the local state schools. The employer could point to evidence that pupils' grades had fallen below the school's normal rate of success. Its subsequent dismissal of a teacher who did not meet the higher standards was fair. Fletcher v. St Leonard's School [1987].

standards were higher than those of similar employers) or someone who could not meet an employer's raised standards could be considered to lack capability for the purposes of the legislation.

Capability must relate to work of the kind that the employee was engaged to carry out. Whether the employee can carry out work or not will be determined on the facts of the case, taking into account the employment contract.

Although conduct and capability are different in origin and will therefore be treated separately, where they arise, they will both be tackled using the disciplinary process.

HR Headmistress tip

Managers often get their language confused when it comes to discipline. For example, I will hear a manager discussing poor timekeeping with an employee and saying 'Your performance has got to improve'. In that case, timekeeping is about an unwillingness to meet the standards – which is conduct. So the employee's conduct related to timekeeping has to improve, rather than his performance. When you're dealing with the law, clarity, precision and consistency are vital.

It is now very common for organisations to have separate polices and procedures for conduct and capability issues. The underpinning law is still the same. There is an example of a policy for managing poor work performance in Appendix 1.

Sometimes it's extremely difficult to determine the real reason why an employee is not meeting your standards. If someone keeps making mistakes on the production line, is it because he's not competent or is it a misconduct matter? If you carry out a thorough investigation this should guide you to the answer.

The law relating to the disciplinary process is principally found in the Advice, Conciliation and Arbitration Service (ACAS) Code of Practice 1 Disciplinary and Grievance procedures 2009, which set out the principles for handling disciplinary and grievance situations in the workplace and gives basic guidance to employers, employees and their companions.

You are expected to know and follow the ACAS Code and accompanying guide; ignorance of the law is no excuse. If you unreasonably fail to follow the Code a tribunal can increase any compensation awarded by up to 25%. Conversely, if the court considers that an employee has unreasonably failed to follow the guidance set out in the Code, it can reduce any award by up to 25%.

The law requires employers to demonstrate fairness and transparency. This can be achieved by using rules and procedures which are clear and specific for handling disciplinary matters. Your disciplinary procedure does not automatically form part of an employment contract so an employee can't claim breach of contract if you fail to follow it. If you choose to make your disciplinary procedure contractual and you fail to follow it when taking disciplinary action, the employee could bring a breach of contract claim against you.

It is important that employees and managers understand what the rules and procedures are, where they can be found and how they are to be used. Disciplinary rules should give examples of acts which the employer regards as acts of gross misconduct or gross incompetence. These may vary according to the nature of the organisation and what it does, but might include things such as theft or fraud, physical violence, gross negligence or serious insubordination.

The ACAS Code identifies a number of points which promote fairness. For example, employers and employees should raise and deal with issues promptly and should not unreasonably delay meetings, decisions or confirmation of those decisions. Both employers and employees should act consistently.

It is important to carry out investigations of potential disciplinary matters without unreasonable delay to establish the facts of the case. In some cases this will require the holding of an investigatory meeting with the employee before proceeding to any disciplinary hearing. In other cases, the investigatory stage will be the collection of evidence by the employer for use at any disciplinary hearing.

If there is an investigatory meeting this should not, by itself, result in any disciplinary action. Although there is no statutory right for an employee to be accompanied at a formal investigatory meeting, such a right may be allowed under your own procedure. If it is, you should follow it.

While there is no legal requirement to do so, the courts have shown an increasing preference for the investigation to be carried out by one person and any subsequent formal meeting to be carried out by another. This is to ensure impartiality. The argument is that if you have investigated and found there is a case to answer, it's very difficult to be impartial as a disciplining office if you have already reached that view. If you are a small business, you can include in a form of words in the discipline procedure which allows the investigating officer to take on the role of disciplining officer. It would be sensible to confine the exercise of a dual role individual to a situation which a) has been agreed by the employee and b) is not at a stage which is likely to lead to dismissal.

It is unusual to suspend an employee for poor performance, but it might occasionally happen where there is a concern about gross incompetence or gross negligence. In cases where a period of suspension with pay is considered necessary, the suspension should be as brief as possible. Suspension is the act of last resort and you should only suspend where there really is no alternative; it should not be a knee-jerk reaction. The Court of Appeal in a case called Mezey v. SW London & St George NHS Trust [2007] made it clear that it considered that suspension is **not** a neutral action. The Court took the view that suspension 'casts a shadow' over the proceedings. I'd suggest that where you have reasonable grounds for belief that the employee's continued presence at work would a) put the employee at risk; b) put others at risk; c) put the organisation at risk (or a combination of any of these), then it would be fair to consider precautionary suspension. Where you do have to suspend make it clear that the suspension is not considered a disciplinary action.

If you decide that there is a disciplinary case to answer, write to the employee to set up a formal meeting. The letter should give details of the time and venue for the disciplinary meeting and advise the employee of his right to be accompanied at the meeting. The companion has the right to help the employee prepare, to address the hearing, present his case, to confer with the worker during the hearing and to sum up. It doesn't give the companion the right to answer on the employee's behalf.

The letter should also contain sufficient information about the alleged poor work performance; this will enable the employee to prepare to answer the case at a disciplinary meeting. It would normally be appropriate to include copies of any written evidence with the notification, this would include witness statements. There is an example of a letter inviting an employee to a formal meeting to discuss poor work performance in Appendix 5.

The meeting should be held without unreasonable delay, whilst allowing the employee reasonable time to prepare his case. It is usual to allow two or three working days preparation time, though it can be longer. If the employee fails to attend without giving a reason, you should reschedule at least once. If the employee is sick, then reschedule and encourage him to attend. However, **you do not have to wait for months for the employee to return**; where the employee is persistently unable or unwilling to attend the meeting, you can make a decision based on the evidence available.

HR Headmistress tip

If the employee goes on sick leave with stress (it does happen quite a lot), leave it for a week or so, and content yourself with writing to say that you are sorry to hear that the employee is sick and hope he will feel better soon. If he continues to be absent from work, convene a welfare meeting. If the employee is able to understand what you're saying and is able to express himself lucidly, he may well be able to attend a formal disciplinary meeting, even if he is signed off from work. If the employee wants you to take medical advice you can do so. Once the matter has been to occupational health advisors, they often say the employee is fit to attend the meeting.

Keep an open mind about this. Not everyone who becomes unwell after being requested to attend a disciplinary meeting is seeking to avoid the issue. The prospect of discipline is upsetting and many cases of discipline-letter-induced stress may be genuine. You can empathise with that, but say that the longer the employee has to wait for the meeting, the tougher it's likely to be on him. You can always make reasonable adjustments to encourage and enable him to attend.

All parties should make every effort to attend the meeting. At the meeting you should explain the complaint against the employee and go through the evidence that has been gathered. The employee should be allowed to set out his case and answer any allegations that have been made. He should be given a reasonable opportunity to ask questions, present evidence and call relevant witnesses. He should also be given an opportunity to raise points about any information provided by witnesses. Where one of the parties intends to call relevant witnesses he should give advance notice of his intentions.

If a formal sanction is needed, the level and nature must be reasonable or justified. This will depend on all the circumstances of the particular case.

Workers have a statutory right to be accompanied by a companion where the disciplinary meeting could result in:

✓ a formal warning being issued
✓ the taking of some other disciplinary action
✓ the confirmation of a warning or some other disciplinary action (such as appeal hearings).

Regarding the companion, I find it's one of most contentious areas. The rights are enshrined words in two pieces of legislation: Section

10 of the Employment Relations Act 1999, which gives the right to be accompanied, and Section 37 of the Employment Relations Act 2004, which gives the companion greater rights.

Section 10 says that the chosen companion may be a fellow worker, a trade union representative, or an official employed by a trade union. A trade union representative who is not an employed official must have been certified by their union as being competent to accompany a worker.

Section 37 gives the companion the right to help the employee prepare, to address the hearing, present his case, to confer with the worker during the hearing and to sum up on his behalf. It doesn't give the companion the right to answer for the employee.

HR Headmistress tip

Where you confine the choice of companion to the statutory pool, but this is being challenged, it can be useful to provide a copy of the sections in the relevant legislation; it prevents arguments. A copy has been provided in Appendix 7.

To exercise the statutory right to be accompanied, workers must make a reasonable request. What is reasonable will depend on the circumstances of each individual case. It would not normally be reasonable for workers to insist on being accompanied by a companion whose presence would prejudice the hearing, nor would it be reasonable for a worker to ask to be accompanied by a companion from a remote geographical location if someone suitable and willing is available on site.

There's no statutory right to be accompanied by a legal advisor, though there have been recent cases where the court agreed that the employee's right to a fair hearing was compromised by the employer's denial of legal representation.

Learning from life's lessons

A patient complained that Dr Kulkarni had acted inappropriately. The Trust investigated and advised him that it intended to carry out a disciplinary hearing. The Trust refused to allow Dr Kulkarni legal representation. He argued unsuccessfully that the circumstances were such that he should be allowed legal representation at the hearing.

Dr Kulkarni argued that as a public authority, the Trust was bound to act in a manner consistent with Article 6 ECHR and that the right to legal representation was a necessary requirement of a fair hearing under Article 6, in appropriate circumstances.

Eventually, the case came before the Court of Appeal, which concluded that, in this case, the claimant had a contractual entitlement to be legally represented at the hearing by a solicitor instructed by his professional body. The employee faced charges of sufficient gravity that, if proved, he would in effect be barred from employment anywhere within the NHS. The existence of a right to present a complaint to the Tribunal was also not enough to cure any lack of fairness in the disciplinary hearings. Kulkarni v. Milton Keynes Hospital NHS Trust [2009].

This is applicable in very limited circumstances and is likely to apply where the consequences of dismissal could not be remedied simply by the making of an unfair dismissal claim.

You may need to make arrangements for an different type of companion where an employee is disabled and might need additional help to participate in the process and present his case.

For example, if an employee is deaf and his first language is British sign language, you may wish to arrange to have a BSL trained interpreter present.

Prevention: setting and communicating standards

The key components of managing performance successfully are:

✓ setting and communicating standards
✓ regular feedback
✓ correction where needed.

Standards are the minimum levels of performance or conduct required by the organisation. They inform every part of our working lives. Some will be set by a third party, for example, the UK Parliament (or a regulatory or industry body) some will be set at a senior corporate level, others will be local. Some standards will be very simple, for example, rules relating to timekeeping or dress code, others will be more complex. It is your job as a manager to make sure that your employees know what your standards are. As a rough guide, if you can't explain in clear, precise and measurable terms what you expect your employees to deliver, then you would be likely to have a problem explaining to an employment tribunal why you have reasonable belief that the dismissed employee was incompetent.

Some examples of the methods you can use to express standards are set out in the examples below. Good practice recommends that employees are involved in the development and review of performance-measurement tools; it gets their approval and helps them to understand what performance standards are expected of them.

I imagine you're reading this because someone who works for you is not performing as well as you would like. You need to communicate clearly what you want him to do so that he knows what is required. I have heard managers say things like 'You must comply with the company's dress code', that's fine as a starting point, but it needs further detail. For example, men must wear business suits with shirts and ties, women must wear business suits or tailored separates. Where requirements are complex, break down the standards into smaller pieces so that you can clearly express, and employees can clearly understand, exactly what it is you want.

Most of us tend to be rather general in our speech. How often have you said 'I'll call you back in five minutes' and then not returned the call for another hour? Yet we know that five minutes and sixty minutes are quite different. Precision in speech is a skill worth learning for managers, but it does take practice.

Managers often object to this, taking the view that the employee 'ought to know', especially if he is experienced, in a skilled profession etc. You really can't assume anything. (As an aside, a colleague once told me 'You'd be surprised how many accountants can't add up on a piece of paper.') Not only do you have to develop clear, precise standards, you have to communicate these to your employees. There are no medals for being a secret squirrel in these circumstances; use every means you can to make sure your employees receive your message about standards in the terms you want them to understand.

HR Headmistress tip

It can be useful to give examples and add description when communicating standards. So rather than saying 'Use the right glass for the wine' you would say 'Use a Paris goblet'.

Going back to my earlier point, even if the employee ought to know of your standards (if in the worst case you go to a tribunal for a capability dismissal) the Employment Judge and other panel members won't know so, at the very least, you might end up having to explain things to them. Check everything, assume nothing and remember – the devil's in the detail!

In order to determine whether an employee is not performing to an acceptable level you have to have some measurable standards in place. Your employees should know what the standards are and what is required of them. The type of measure used will vary from role to role. Some examples of measurement tools are described in the following paragraphs:

A detailed job description which sets out the outputs/outcomes of the role may be a useful measurement tool. Discuss this with your employee and keep him regularly updated to reflect changes in outputs/outcomes required. Job descriptions are for guidance. They are not contractual. They don't have to be complicated. There are three parts to a job description:

✓ job title
✓ summary of the main purpose of the job
✓ key tasks, of which one point is always 'any other reasonable management request'.

The use of pre-set targets which are realistic and achievable can help you to determine whether an employee is achieving the standard required of him. Pre-set targets are often used in sales roles.

Quality controls may be useful where the provision of a quality service is essential, for example, customer-facing roles or quality assurance. Quality controls/measures could include a review of the nature and level of complaints received, observation of the employee and a review and discussion of previous performance.

Learning from life's lessons

A manager had to give some correction to an employee who was producing technical reports for a client. The reports didn't meet the manager's standard in terms of written English and he wondered how to approach the employee. This is the feedback he gave:

'When we write or review these polices, not only do we have to get the technical stuff right, it's a good opportunity to clarify and clean up the English and grammar. The aim, therefore, is to ensure that sentences are complete, proper nouns are used consistently and correctly, we avoid inappropriate or unnecessary repetition and use fairly simple English. The vast majority of people who read regularly in the UK read tabloids, i.e. they are pitched at a reading age of about ten, so it's essential to use simple, straightforward language.

When reviewing documents I always find it helpful to do the work, put it aside, then print off and read the documents before sending. It's much easier to spot mistakes – something to do with physical definition on the screen I believe. For example, there was a reference to a partner in the documents you sent me which you had not picked up. ABC co. is a limited company, so there are no partners, but it's so easily missed when you only check on screen.'

The manager chatted this through with the employee. Amongst other things, it turned out that the employee didn't know what proper nouns were. This wasn't entirely surprising as there have been several generations of school children who haven't been taught grammar at school to a sufficient level. By discussing the standards with the employee in an objective fashion, the problem was quickly remedied.

Some companies set standards by using a competency framework. Competency frameworks focus on the key behaviours required to achieve competent performance. They can be helpful in identifying which aspects of the employee's performance are not yet up to standard. This will typically include a list of relevant competencies with definitions and behavioural indicators or statements of what each looks like in action.

Make sure that you introduce key standards at the earliest possible stage; this may be recruitment, where you are involved in it, or induction.

Ensure that the employee has been trained to do the work you're asking him to do. It is completely unreasonable to criticise someone for poor work performance if he hasn't got the skills for the job. The example on the following page demonstrates this.

Learning from life's lessons

Steelprint Ltd was a printing company specialising in the marketing and printing of small, self-adhesive address labels. Ms Haynes started working for them in April 1989 as an order clerk. Originally she worked in the proof room department. Ms Haynes contract stated that 'It is a condition of your employment that you are fully flexible with your approach to working practices and hours.' The main work of entering orders which were received was in fact done in the main office building. Although Ms Hayne's job title was order clerk, 80% of her work was proof reading. This continued for nearly five years without, apparently, any relevant complaint from the employer as to the way in which she performed her duties.

From January 1994, the employer made widespread changes in their organisation to adapt to competition and computerisation, including a restructuring of the order clerks department. Ms Haynes and eight other order clerks were moved to the main building and the work content of their jobs was changed. In addition to proof reading she was now required to undertake the inputting of orders into the new computer system. To do this, she had to be able to touch type. She couldn't master the new skill. There was a period of monitoring and the employer issued her with several formal warnings over a three-month period. Ms Haynes failed to meet the speed and accuracy targets for inputting information and was dismissed. She complained successfully that her dismissal was unfair. The main reason was that the employer had not provided her with training, nor did it consider moving her to other tasks to which she might be better suited. Steelprint Ltd. v. Haynes [1996].

Prevention:
regular feedback

Managing performance is all about giving feedback on a regular basis. In addition to the exchanges that take place during the working day, it is also useful to meet with employees regularly to discuss how things are going and to give and receive feedback informally.

These meetings are useful for reiterating performance standards, clarifying understanding, providing relevant information, and establishing agreements and expectations on both sides. They can be very helpful in nipping problems in the bud. To be most effective, they should take place every two or three months.

HR Headmistress tip

In order to make the conversation as useful, accurate and as relevant as possible, note down points for discussion on a weekly basis.

These may already be matters you have discussed with the employee, but there's no harm in revisiting them. A balanced approach is important, so your notes should include things that you are pleased about as well as any areas which need improvement.

You will find a checklist setting out the principles of effective feedback in Appendix 2.

What goes wrong?

Capability issues can arise for a variety of reasons. Causes of poor work performance include:

✓ inadequate or insufficient training

✓ poor systems of work, out-of-date policies or inadequate procedures that do not encourage efficient or effective work

✓ tools and equipment that don't work properly or frequently break down

✓ poor quality or inadequate supervision and/or support

✓ lack of understanding on the employee's part about his job duties, priorities or goals, which may arise because no one has properly explained these issues or given the employee feedback

✓ unclear instructions

✓ work overload, causing stress and fatigue

✓ unrealistic targets or deadlines that are virtually impossible for the employee to achieve

✓ poor working relationships causing the employee worry, upset or stress

✓ bullying or harassment

✓ physical or mental ill health, for example where the employee's state of health, or medication taken to deal with it, is causing tiredness

✓ personal problems that would inevitably affect the employee's concentration.

None of these issues will be the employee's fault. Most fall within your control.

What about a situation where an employee has the necessary skills and abilities to perform the role but is not doing so and there is a resultant decline in his performance?

Before deciding what action to take, find out why the employee is behaving in this manner, for example:

✓ Is the employee demotivated? If so, why?
✓ Is the role very routine or repetitive? Can it be enhanced or rotated?
✓ Does the employee have any personal problems which are affecting him?
✓ Are there any conflict issues which could be impacting on his work?

Considering factors such as these can help you to decide the best way to tackle the problem. If an employee is demotivated because of, for example, a lack of feedback or recognition or because he has difficulties in his personal life, disciplinary action is not likely to lead to any improvement.

If you are satisfied that there are no internal or external circumstances impacting on the employee's motivation then follow the procedure set out in the section entitled 'Cure: informal management'.

Cure:
informal management

Take appropriate action as soon as you notice that the employee is not performing work to the required standard. Delaying, or worse, doing nothing, may well cause the performance problem to get worse. The result of this could be that you have to face a major crisis caused by underperformance rather than dealing with the problem while it is still in its infancy. The investigation checklist in Appendix 3 gives you a range of useful prompts.

Investigating will help you put together an accurate picture of the employee's performance and identify which, if any, external factors could be affecting him. The first steps will be informal. Many managers worry about conducting a meeting with an employee to discuss unsatisfactory performance, even when it's informal. In order to make the meeting as effective as possible:

✓ stick to facts and avoid expressing personal opinions
✓ be specific, avoiding vague, woolly statements
✓ avoid generalisations, for example, 'You're always making mistakes'
✓ ask open questions
✓ listen actively to what the employee has to say and take it on board
✓ ensure that your tone is friendly and not accusatory
✓ use positive words such as 'improvement' and 'achievement', rather than negative words such as 'failure' or 'weakness'
✓ focus the discussion on future improvement rather than on past inadequacies
✓ always check for understanding, for example, by asking the employee to state or summarise his understanding of what you have discussed.

There is a checklist setting the points you need to cover at an informal discussion in Appendix 4.

HR Headmistress tip

Some managers flounder because they're not quite sure what words to use. I have heard many inexperienced managers say somewhat regrettable things like:

'Why are you so lazy?', 'Why are your widgets always wonky?', 'Your cupcakes are the worst in the department.'

Believe me, managers do say this sort of thing. You won't be surprised to learn that statements like these will only antagonise all but the most self-effacing employees (and you don't see too many in that bracket these days), so you need to practice learning to use objective language and separate the person from the performance.

Mahatma Ghandi is credited with the phrase 'Hate the sin, love the sinner'. The sentiment applies neatly to the management of poor work performance. The table on the following page shows some examples of what to say and – perhaps even more importantly – what not to say.

Don't say	Do say
You're always making mistakes.	There are three mistakes in this piece of work.
You tend to shout at people.	I noticed at last week's meeting that you shouted rather loudly at Louise when she...
You're hopeless – you never meet your deadlines.	You've missed the monthly deadline six times this year so far, on each occasion by at least two days.
You're very aggressive.	I appreciate that you may not realise this, but sometimes your tone and manner come across to others as aggressive. For example...
Your work is not up to scratch. You'll have to pull your socks up.	This piece of work falls short of the standard we require because...
You're lazy. I can't ever rely on you to complete a piece of work.	It has been brought to my attention that you have not completed...
You have a lousy attitude towards the rest of the staff.	What do you think you could do to improve your working relationship with your colleagues?

Sometimes when you start talking to an employee about poor work performance, he might make remarks about or blame you. If he does, keep your head and don't allow yourself to become defensive otherwise the conversation will go off track. It would be better to defer responding to such comments until you have time to consider them. The comments may be valid.

There is no right to be accompanied at an informal meeting. You may wish to allow an employee to have a companion in certain circumstances, for example, if:

✓ the employee is a young person (below the age of 18)
✓ the employee has a disability that impacts on his ability to understand and participate in the process
✓ the employee does not speak English as his first language.

The whole point of this discussion is to guide the employee to the standard you require, so provide clear, precise guidance and write it down for the employee.

Learning from life's lessons

Peter owns and runs a shoot. He'd experienced problems with one of his gamekeepers, Mick. Over the last year Peter had several discussions with Mick about the quality of his work. Peter had detailed his concerns and given Mick examples of where he believed Mick had fallen below the standards. The discussions had been confirmed in writing.

Mick asked Peter for more time to settle into his job and Peter agreed to that. Six months later, Peter still had serious concerns about Mick's work performance. When Peter inspected Mick's beat, he found that in some places feed hoppers had been taken away or were empty. On others, there were an excessive number of feed hoppers for the size of the area.

After an investigation it became clear that although, Mick was a qualified keeper, he didn't understand that there has to be a minimum ratio of food hoppers to number of birds (pheasants don't queue up for food; if it's not there they wander away, with a consequent loss of profit to the business owner). After investigating and discussing the matter, Peter gave the following written guidance to Mick.

1. You will need to ensure that you have enough food hoppers. The general rule is one hopper to thirty birds. The hoppers should be placed fifteen to twenty yards apart. Please review the number of birds to be raised against the number of hoppers and provide PS with the number of hoppers you will require by next Monday.

2. You must not use a paint tin (or any other containers that have previously held or stored chemicals) to distribute either food or water. Ensure you use a bucket which is clean, in good repair and only used for this purpose.

After you've had a discussion with the employee, the next stage is to create a performance improvement plan (PIP). How do you go about writing a PIP? The first step is to agree and set down precise performance targets which are capable of being measured. People respond best to raising the bar little by little, so setting down targets that can be increased incrementally can work well. Write down the levels of performance to achieve and the time limit within which the targets should be met. Be very clear about what you want and what constitutes success. I cannot sufficiently emphasise the importance of being precise. If you're not very detailed, it can come back to bite you.

Learning from life's lessons

One of my favourite 'how-not-to-get-the-detail-right' lessons is the story of Doris. Doris was a long standing employee and an excellent worker, but she had chronic Monday-itis. She'd had 20 days off in a three month period. Enough was enough and her manager, Susan, took her aside and explained that she was worried about Doris' health. Doris confirmed that she had no underlying health problems. Susan asked what the company could do to support Doris and enable her to attend for work more often. Doris said there was nothing (all good stuff so far!). Susan went on to say that Doris had to improve her levels of attendance as they were unacceptably poor. They would meet again in three months to review Doris' attendance. If Doris hadn't improved by that time, said Susan, she would have to consider taking disciplinary action on the grounds of Doris' poor attendance.

Three months later they met again ... and Doris had only taken 18 days off. Susan had got what she asked for, but not what she wanted.

Once you have both agreed your precise improvements, apply the following:

✓ Agree a process to keep both of you informed of progress and diarise follow-ups.

✓ If the employee needs any training, specify that in the PIP.

✓ Build in a date for an interim performance evaluation to assess the employee's progress.

✓ Include the employee's suggestions in the PIP.

✓ List the positive outcomes of successfully completing the performance improvement plan along with the negative consequences of failing to meet performance criteria.

✓ Ask the employee to date and sign the PIP, acknowledging that he has read and understands its requirements. There is an example of a PIP in Appendix 8.

✓ Note that the process of encouraging the employee to improve his performance starts at the informal stage. If it becomes necessary to escalate to the formal process, the PIP will continue to run in parallel with any formal sanctions.

✓ Review at weekly intervals, so you keep track of progress. If the situation picks up and the employee starts to perform better, this will be encouraging for both of you. Give accurate and targeted feedback. Try to focus on the positive as this will increase motivation and performance.

✓ Give enough time for the employee to improve; this should be at least one - three months, but it does depend on the circumstances. If in doubt give more time rather than less.

Cure:
formal process

If the employee's work performance doesn't improve after informal guidance, then you may need to move to a more formal structure.

HR Headmistress tip

Allow an employee reasonable time to improve and have two or maybe three informal discussions with him. After that, escalate the matter to the formal process. If you end up having fifty informal chats, you can tell the informal approach isn't working.

The formal process continues to try to identify the reasons for, and barriers to, poor work performance and tries to provide support so that the employee can make the necessary improvements.

Start by writing to the employee requesting him to attend a formal meeting. Include details of the standards required, the actual performance delivered and evidence supporting your view that there is a case to answer. You can refer to earlier informal conversations, so long as they are relatively recent. A sample letter requesting an employee to attend a formal meeting is in Appendix 5.

Make sure that this employee is not being singled out. Is his performance measurably worse than others who are not subject to discipline? If there's a broader problem you'll need to address it with the group.

To ensure that any disciplinary interview is carried out effectively and fairly it is essential to take the following actions:

✓ Consider all the facts of the case.

✓ Tell the employee about the complaint made against him.

✓ Check all the evidence submitted by others. Obtain all witness statements well in advance.

✓ Give the employee sufficient time to prepare a response to the allegations. ACAS recommend up to five working days, but it doesn't have to be that long.

✓ Involve full-time union officials whenever disciplinary action involves trade union representatives.

✓ Ensure that disciplinary meetings are carried out at a location which is suitable for the purpose and free from interruptions.

✓ While you're not bound by precedent, you should be aware of the types of disciplinary action taken in the past in similar circumstances.

✓ Never conduct formal meetings alone. Arrange to be accompanied by someone capable of acting as a witness and taking notes.

✓ Conduct the meeting in a calm, structured way, making notes of the points to be covered.

✓ Hold the interview and give the employee every opportunity to explain matters.

✓ Take time to check the explanations where possible. Have documentation and witnesses available.

✓ At the end of the meeting summarise the main points. Investigate any additional areas that need to be checked. If necessary adjourn during the meeting to check information.

✓ It is sensible to take your time at the end of the meeting to review your decision. A hasty announcement of any disciplinary penalty makes it look as though it was predetermined.

✓ Always inform the employee of the outcome including:

🖉 the reason for the decision

🖉 the action being taken

🖉 the specific improvement required of the employee

    🖊 the time-scale in which the improvement must take place

    🖊 the duration of any warning

    🖊 how the improvement is to be measured

    🖊 fix a review date.

✓ Confirmation of disciplinary penalties must be given in writing to the employee.

✓ Ensure that the employee is given full details of how to lodge an appeal against the decision.

✓ An explanation must be given of the next stage of the proceedings if there is a failure to improve.

✓ There is an example of a formal warning letter in Appendix 6.

HR Headmistress tip

If an employee wants to resign rather than face dismissal you can accept a resignation up until the formal hearing starts. Don't accept a resignation tendered part way through the disciplinary hearing. You could be accused of duress and then face a possible constructive unfair dismissal claim. Continue with the hearing. If the employee gets up and walks out, adjourn the hearing and write to the employee to reconvene it. If he fails to attend you can complete it in his absence.

Where the employee is found to be performing unsatisfactorily it is usual to give him a first-stage formal warning. A further failure to improve performance within a set period would normally result in a second or final warning (depending on how many stages you have in your procedure).

The law doesn't stipulate the length of warnings, although the convention is for the first warning to be of six months' duration and second/final warnings to be of 12 months' duration. In exceptional cases I might award a warning of 24 months' duration, but that's the maximum I'd set. Ultimately, it's a question for the employer to address, and is subject to the usual requirement of reasonableness. The usual rule is that you do not dismiss for a first breach of poor performance. Most errors are likely to be small but persistent; however, if an employee's first unsatisfactory performance is sufficiently serious, it may be appropriate to move directly to a final warning. This might occur where the employee's actions have had, or are liable to have, a serious or harmful impact on the organisation. Cost in and of itself is not usually sufficient to merit dismissal for a first breach.

Generally, employees dismissed for poor performance are not being dismissed for gross incompetence and therefore should be paid their contractual notice at termination. This will usually be attract tax and national insurance deductions.

Learning from life's lessons

Printers Diemer and Reynolds Ltd had designed a procedure to ensure that the gathering of various sections of a book was done properly and in the right order. Mr Day was employed as a print operator. He did not follow the procedure and, in consequence, 7,000 books in the print run were faulty and had to be scrapped. Mr Day was dismissed and complained that his dismissal was unfair. The tribunal agreed and said that the sanction of dismissal was completely disproportionate to the employee's mistake. Day v. Diemer and Reynolds Ltd [1975].

Some acts are so serious in themselves, or have such serious consequences, that they may call for dismissal without notice for a first offence. You must still ensure that you follow a fair disciplinary process, before dismissing for gross incompetence. The general rule is that an employee with less than 51 weeks' service cannot bring a claim for unfair dismissal, though he can make a complaint of breach of contract if you don't comply with a contractual disciplinary procedure.

Note that there are a number of situations where the employee is protected against unfair dismissal even where his service is less than 51 weeks. The moral of the story is to follow a fair, but shortened process in the first year.

If you decide to issue a formal warning, explain the nature of the poor performance and explain how long the warning will remain current. Advise the employee of the consequences of a failure to improve performance, within the set period following a final warning. For instance, that it may result in dismissal or some other contractual penalty such as demotion or loss of seniority. A decision to dismiss should only be taken by a manager who has the authority to do so. Tell the employee as soon as possible what the reasons for the dismissal are, the date on which the employment contract will end, the appropriate period of notice and his right of appeal.

If, following a series of formal warnings and the provision of the required support to improve, the employee's performance has remained at a level that is clearly unsatisfactory, you may be able to dismiss the employee fairly. Dismissal for a lack of capability is a potentially fair reason for dismissal. Don't rush into it though. Dismissal for poor work performance will be unfair if you have not first taken the appropriate steps to give the employee an opportunity, and sufficient time, to improve to the standard required.

Learning from life's lessons

Mr Taylor was a commercial pilot. He forgot to put down the undercarriage of his plane when landing. Seventy seven passengers were on board and there were reasonable weather conditions. No one was hurt, but the aircraft sustained considerable damage. Following an inquiry and a disciplinary hearing, Mr Taylor was dismissed. He had never had an accident before and his competence had never previously been called into question. He complained that he had been unfairly dismissed. The case eventually went to the Court of Appeal. The Court agreed with the employer that even though he had not made any mistakes before, Mr Taylor's mistake was fundamental incompetence warranting summary dismissal. In this case the Court said that, where the level of competence required was particularly high, and the consequences of any deviation from that level of competence could be exceptionally serious, in certain cases, such as this, it would be fair to dismiss for a first offence. Alidair Ltd v. Taylor [1978].

There was a different result in British Midland Airways Ltd v. Gilmore [1981]. Here a pilot in similar circumstances was only told of the charges against him at the disciplinary hearing and had no idea that he was at risk of dismissal, unlike Mr Taylor, who was kept fully informed. The court said that, even though death to passengers could result from incompetence, the employer could not dispense with the standard disciplinary procedures.

It is usual for two or three warnings to be given before dismissal is contemplated. The courts take the view that it is an extremely serious matter to deprive a person of his livelihood, so you are expected to give plenty of time for the employee to improve.

Alidair v. Taylor is an extreme case. The risk is a risk that is too great for an employer to accept. In this case, the employer would not take the risk of a repetition occurring. One airplane crash was enough to trigger a fair dismissal.

Dismissal is, of course, the ultimate sanction and an act of last resort. If you dismiss an employee on the grounds of incompetence, the onus is on you to show that this is the real reason for the dismissal.

This means that you will have to produce evidence of the employee's poor performance and show that this was the real reason for the dismissal.

In order to dismiss, it is enough that you have reasonable grounds for belief that the employee is not competent. Referring once again to Alidair v. Taylor, Lord Denning gave the following guidance to employers:

'Whenever a man is dismissed for incapacity or incompetence it is sufficient that the employer honestly believes on reasonable grounds that the man is incapable and incompetent. It is **not necessary** for the employer to **prove** that he is in fact incapable or incompetent'(my use of bold).

Tribunals will take all surrounding circumstances into account and you always have to show that the actions you take are reasonable and proportionate in the circumstances.

You might think that if an employee doesn't hit his targets or quota (it might be sales, numbers of widgets, number of calls etc.) then there would be grounds for dismissal (as long as the procedure has been properly followed). It probably will, but remember that the employment tribunals tend to work to a very different timescale to the rest of us. Most managers want the employee to demonstrate competence in two weeks, where two months – or longer – is going to be far more realistic.

Employees who have received a formal sanction have the right to appeal against the decision. You should confirm the details in writing (i.e. to whom the appeal should be made, in what format and by what date). Employees should let employers know the grounds for their appeal in writing. Appeals should be heard without unreasonable delay and, ideally, at an agreed time and place. One stage of appeal will satisfy the ACAS Code.

The appeal should be dealt with impartially and, wherever possible, by a manager who has not previously been involved in the case. Workers have a statutory right to be accompanied at appeal hearings and employees should be informed in writing of the results of the appeal hearing and the reasons for the decision as soon as possible. By giving reasons for the decision, it may dissuade an employee from bringing a frivolous claim in the employment tribunal.

Where disciplinary action is being considered against an employee who is a trade union representative, the normal disciplinary procedure should be followed. Depending on the circumstances, it is procedure to discuss the matter at an early stage with an official employed by the union, after obtaining the employee's agreement.

I just want to raise one final point. These days many employees raise a grievance during the disciplinary process. Many employers think that the ACAS Code requires them to postpone the disciplinary process until the grievance is resolved. It doesn't. Paragraph 44 says:

'Where an employee raises a grievance during the disciplinary process the disciplinary process may be temporarily suspended in order to deal with the grievance. Where the grievance and disciplinary cases are related it may be appropriate to deal with both cases concurrently.'

In the case of Samuel Smith Old Brewery (Tadcaster) v. Marshall and another [2010], Mr and Mrs Marshall, a husband and wife team, were joint pub managers. The brewery required them to reduce additional staffing hours. In response, they submitted a grievance, arguing that this would mean they were required to work an unacceptable number of hours themselves. At the grievance hearing the brewery confirmed its instructions and did not uphold their grievance. The Marshalls refused to comply and appealed against the grievance decision. The brewery started the disciplinary process. At a disciplinary hearing, which took place one week prior to the grievance appeal hearing was due to take place, it dismissed both Mr and Mrs Marshall for gross misconduct. The Marshalls claimed unfair dismissal.

On appeal, the Employment Appeal Tribunal found that it had not been necessary for the brewery to complete the entire grievance procedure (including appeal) before conducting the disciplinary hearing. It held that only in the rarest of cases would it be outside the range of reasonable responses for an employer to proceed with a disciplinary process before hearing a grievance appeal. Such rare cases might include where there was some clear evidence of unfairness or prejudice which cannot otherwise be compensated for. This was not a case where there had been no grievance hearing at all and this counted in the brewery's favour.

The court went on to say that if the employees had attended the disciplinary hearing, they could have raised the points they intended to raise at the forthcoming grievance appeal. In the absence of some clear unfairness or prejudice to an employee, it will only be in rare circumstances that an employer may not continue with a disciplinary process before holding a grievance appeal meeting. However, where there is clear evidence of unfairness or prejudice, an employer should hear a grievance appeal first.

HR Headmistress tip

If an employee raises a grievance in response to the disciplinary process and is not likely to be dismissed, I tend to deal with the process by holding a grievance meeting, adjourning and having a short break, then convening the disciplinary meeting. Where the employee is likely to be dismissed, I would complete the grievance process first.

Management of poor work performance v. harassment

When an employee does not demonstrate competence you have relatively few options as an employer. It boils down to trying to help him correct his performance informally or formally, or doing nothing. The latter option is not recommended.

Many employers hesitate to start the process of managing poor work performance because they fear they will be accused of bullying the employee. The law seems to assume that when you start the process of correction (and that is after all what the disciplinary process is about) that the employee will meekly cooperate, immediately promising to work harder and more diligently, a touch of the 'You can rely on me, Guv'nor' tripping off his tongue.

Although this somewhat Victorian fantasy response may well happen, it just as often does not. My experience is that employee defensiveness in the face of quite mild corrective coaching seems to be very common now. Sometimes this is really quite aggressive. As a consequence, a manager may find himself the subject of a grievance citing bullying and harassment, simply because he is trying to do his job. In the face of this type of behaviour (or in anticipation of it), many managers simply let the whole thing go hang. On a human level, I can quite see why. But if you're running a business or managing a team, you can't afford to ignore poor work performance.

So what do you do if an employee complains of harassment when you're trying to manage him? There are a number of tactics. Make sure that your dignity at work procedure points out that managers have a right and a duty to manage. If a manager is seeking to help and encourage an employee to do his job, it does not constitute bullying, harassment or victimisation.

It is easier to attack than defend. Some employees create such a stink with their complaints that managers fear the consequences of tackling poor performance. Be well-prepared to provide evidence of poor work performance to support what you say. Ask why the employee thinks he is being bullied. A useful phrase to bring out is 'Help me understand why you think I'm treating you less favourably than anyone else who performs at this level?' Then wait politely for the answer. Repeat if necessary. By putting the onus back on the employee you start to call him to account. That's what happened in the next example on the following page.

It is my experience that when you start to properly manage performance, the employee will respond in one of four ways described below.

✓ He will shape up and make efforts to reach the required standard – this is what we want to happen.

✓ If an employee can't, or won't, reach the standard it is quite common for him to leave of his own volition.

✓ Sometimes employees come to you and ask to go on terms i.e., he asks you to make him a payment to leave the organization. If you do this, it's best to arrange for the employee to sign a legally binding compromise agreement. This means that in return for a sum of money, he compromises his right to go to employment tribunal. You do need to make sure that the terms of the compromise agreement are properly drafted.

✓ The last option is for the employee to carry on as before and be managed out through the formal process. We will consider formal disciplinary action if it becomes necessary and dismissal is the action of last resort. Managing through the formal process is quite unusual; I almost never have to dismiss anyone.

Learning from life's lessons

Warren was employed by a company as a programmer and software developer. His performance was poor. He had about two years' service, but his manager, James, had never really given clear direction to him that he was not meeting the standards.

Time passed and Warren's performance got worse. Things came to a head when one afternoon, James was with a client trying to complete the final stages of a project. It became clear that the code Warren was supposed to have written and tested didn't work. It was a supremely embarrassing moment. James extricated himself with as much grace as he could, apologising profusely to the client. He got back to the office and, having got past the urge to say or do something regrettable, decided to start the process to manage the matter formally.

The company convened a disciplinary hearing. You might expect that Warren would have been embarrassed by the failure of his code. He wasn't. It was everyone else's fault, he said. He hadn't had training, James didn't explain things properly, nothing to do with me, not my fault ...

There was no evidence to support Warren's argument. Nobody else had been involved in the fiasco, James' guidance was detailed to the point of pedantry (and had included asking Warren if he needed any help) and Warren had attended every course that he had needed for the purpose of being competent to do his job. Despite there being considerable evidence of Warren's incompetence, the company decided not take any formal action at that stage, but to put Warren on a performance improvement plan (PIP).

Learning from life's lessons cont.

The company made further arrangements and things settled down. Within a month it was clear that Warren was not following the PIP and things were going wrong. After a further problem, the company decided to start the formal discipline process. He was given a first-stage warning. Warren registered his wish to appeal against the decision and, at the same time, put in a grievance for bullying and harassment against the disciplining manager, his manager, the HR manager – just about everyone involved, in fact.

At this point I was asked to come in to chair the appeal and grievance meetings. Warren decided he didn't like that either. He made a demand for six months pay and good references to go and then went off sick. To start with it was vomiting and diarrhoea, but the condition had mysteriously changed to six months pay and good references and then went off on sick leave. To start with it was vomiting and diarrhoea, but the condition had mysteriously changed to workplace stress by the following week.

The company invoked its right to pay Statutory Sick Pay (SSP) only where someone becomes sick immediately before, during, or after the disciplinary or grievance procedures had been engaged.

After threatening that we had made an unlawful deduction by paying SSP rather than company sick pay, Warren discovered that we were quite within our rights. This calmed him down and brought him back to the negotiating table. Once that had happened, we were able to reach a conclusion that was reasonable and affordable to the company, but just sufficient to allow him to agree and go away. The matter was then compromised and closed.

It's important to remember that employees also have a duty to do what they reasonably can to comply with performance requirements and to address themselves wholeheartedly to performance improvement plans. If an under-performing employee refuses to do so, expressly or tacitly, and starts making allegations of harassment and bullying as a way of deflecting attention from himself, I would be inclined to move to the formal process sooner rather than later.

Learning how to deal with underperformance is an essential management skill. It takes time and patience, but it's not difficult. By following and practising the processes set out in this book, you will master the skills and gain the confidence to apply them successfully. As a result you'll find that your team will deliver improved performance, cutting costs, reducing errors and improving productivity.

And that's a big win for you.

Appendices

Appendices

Appendix 1:
Sample capability policy

Purpose

This procedure is designed to deal with those cases where the employee is lacking in some area of knowledge, skill or ability, resulting in a failure to be able to carry out the required duties to an acceptable standard. It is to be used where there is a genuine lack of capability, rather than a deliberate failure on the part of the employee to perform to the standards of which he is capable (for which, use of the disciplinary procedure is appropriate). A genuine lack of capability may have been present for some time or may have come about more recently because of, for example, changing job content or personal factors affecting the individual's performance.

Where an employee is unable to perform all or part of his job for a health-related reason, the Sickness Absence Procedure will be used.

The procedure seeks to:

✓ assist the employee to improve his performance, wherever possible, where such deficiencies exist

✓ provide a firm-but-fair and consistent means of dealing with capability problems without employing the disciplinary procedure

✓ provide a means of solving capability problems where improvement in the current job is not possible.

Application

The procedure applies to all employees other than the Chief Executive and employees who are still on probation.

Informal assistance

Nothing in this procedure is intended to prevent the normal process of supervision control, whereby managers allocate work, monitor performance, draw attention to errors and poor quality and highlight work done well. This may include informal assistance in achieving improvement. Such methods are not part of the formal performance management procedure and, therefore, formal interviews and the right to a companion are not appropriate to this everyday process. Managers should maintain personal notes of difficulties encountered, assistance given and any remedial actions taken for future reference in case formal action is needed; the employee is entitled to have a copy of such notes.

Companion
At all stages of the formal procedure an employee is entitled to have a companion present, who may be a fellow employee or trade union representative. It will be made clear in advance to the employee (and to the companion, if the employee exercises this option) that the performance-management, rather than the disciplinary, procedure is being used.

If at any stage a manager has reason to believe that the non-capability is due to poor conduct or lack of effort on the part of the employee, he will stop the process and may set up a disciplinary interview at a later date in accordance with that procedure. He will inform the employee clearly of the change of procedure and repeat that there is a right to a companion if this has not previously been taken up.

The procedure
In each case, the employee will be given written notification of the matters to be discussed at the meeting at least forty eight hours in advance of the meeting.

Stage 1: Formal Counselling

Where an employee is failing to perform to an acceptable standard, despite having been given informal guidance and assistance, a formal counselling session will be arranged with him by his manager. This is the first stage of the formal process. During this counselling, the employee will be told clearly of the issues which have been identified and precisely of the required improvement in work standard, with the possible consequences of not doing so. There must be an opportunity for the employee to answer these points and to explain any difficulties he may be having, and a discussion on the ways and means by which the desired improvement may be achieved. Appropriate possibilities include:

✓ training, either external or internal

✓ working under closer supervision from a manager, or a work colleague who is competent and experienced in the work for an agreed specified period

✓ agreed changes in duties, either permanently or for a trial period.

The conclusions from this counselling session will be formally recorded in writing, with a copy given to the employee.

A reasonable timescale for improvement will be set (the length to be determined by individual circumstances, but normally not longer than two months), with monitoring during that period and a review meeting at the end of it. If the desired improvement has been achieved, this will be recorded and the employee will be given a copy of the file note.

Stage 2: Final warning

If at the review stage the employee's performance has not met the agreed standard, then a formal meeting will be held. The employee's manager will write to him setting out his concerns and advising him of his right to be accompanied by a work colleague or a trade union representative.

At the meeting the employee will be informed that his performance has not improved to the accepted satisfactory standard. The meeting should consider targets, training, support and review dates, and service requirements in the light of progress made since the informal interview. The meeting will discuss possible options open to the employee including a revised performance improvement agreement, or the option of redeployment to a more suitable post where available.

The review meeting will be followed by a formal letter to the employee setting out the continued deficiencies, the expected improvement, the timescale for achieving it, the further help which will be given, any agreed changes to the employment contract and that a failure to achieve the improvement within the timescale will necessitate a consideration of whether to dismiss from the company's service. The written warning will normally remain live for a six-month period. It will also set out the employee's right of appeal, including to whom the appeal should be made and the time limit for doing so.

A reasonable timescale for improvements will be set (again, normally not longer than two months), with monitoring during that period and a review meeting at the end of it. If the desired improvement has been achieved, this will be recorded and the employee will be given a copy of the file note.

Stage 3: Dismissal

If the employee still has not achieved the required standard of performance and:

✓ there is no suitable alternative employment, or

✓ the employee has refused a reasonable job offer, or

✓ the employee has been redeployed but fails to perform satisfactorily in that post

✓ then a decision to dismiss may be taken

A meeting will be arranged and chaired by a senior manager. The fact of, and reasons for, this termination, the last date of employment, any necessary administrative or financial arrangements, and to whom, and within what time limit, any appeal should be made, will immediately be confirmed to the employee in writing.

Appeals

The right to appeal exists at all stages of the formal procedure. There will not be a delay in implementing management decisions pending the appeal, but they may be subsequently reversed as a result of the appeal hearing.

Appeals must be lodged within seven working days of receipt of either a warning or termination of employment letter, and the appeal hearing would normally take place within the next fifteen working days (unless the parties agree to a delay). The employee has the same right to be accompanied at an appeal as during the above formal stages.

Appeals against decisions of line managers will be chaired by the function head, those against decisions of a function head by the Chief Executive. Appeals against decisions of the Chief Executive will be heard by another function head. In each case an HR advisor will sit with the manager chairing the meeting.

The procedure at appeal hearings will be the same as for formal grievance hearings, except that the management case will be heard first and the employee's second.

Capability of function heads

The principles and procedures in the preceding paragraphs apply to managers and function heads as much as to other employees, but the stages in their cases will need to be undertaken at different levels. For managers, all stages within the procedure will be undertaken by their function head, with appeals being heard by the Chief Executive. The Chief Executive will handle all capability issues in relation to function heads, with appeals to a board member.

Redeployment

Where an employee agrees to redeployment he will have a trial period of six weeks to enable him to try out the new post, with management discretion to extend the period to twelve weeks. The employee's performance will be carefully monitored and assessed during the six weeks. If, during this time, the employee is not satisfied with the job, or the manager does not feel that the performance is adequate or is unlikely to become so, dismissal will be considered.

Appendix 2:
Checklist: giving effective feedback

✓ When you plan your meetings, be clear about your intention. Are you trying to praise, pass on an observation or correct something you think is going wrong? Make sure the timing is right so that the employee is receptive to what you have to say. Hold the conversation in private.

✓ Be precise and specific, for example, 'There is an error rate of 20% in the widgets you are making', rather than 'The widgets you make are rubbish'.

✓ Be helpful and direct the conversation positively, for example, 'Have you tried dealing with the most difficult calls first thing in the morning?'

✓ Where appropriate, help the employee think through the impact of the behaviour about which you are concerned. For example, 'How do you think Jane felt when you …'

✓ Consider what language you will use to convey your message. Use objective language and examples to illustrate your point. Avoid parental language, for example, 'You're *always* the slowest, you *never* take enough care …' It tends to have the effect of making employees resort to childish resistance.

✓ Demonstrate understanding of the other person, as appropriate. For example, 'I know your father has been ill. Are you finding it difficult to get enough rest?'

✓ Focus on the future because you can't change what has already happened.

✓ Keep a record of what has been said.

✓ Follow up, where necessary, to review any actions agreed.

Appendix 3:
Checklist: carrying
out an investigation

When reviewing the situation you must consider all the relevant issues, for example, witness statements, documentary evidence and training records.

The following questions provide some prompts, but it is not an exhaustive list:

✓ What is the employee alleged to have done or failed to do?
✓ Is the poor performance due to misconduct or lack of ability?
✓ Is the person aware that his performance is poor?
✓ How long has the employee been underperforming?
✓ What are the circumstances involved? What happened? When did it happen? Who was involved? Where did the incident occur?
✓ Are environmental conditions a factor affecting performance?
✓ What job was being done by the employee? Is it his usual job?
✓ What is the age and length of service of the employee?
✓ How long has the employee been in his present job?
✓ Has the job changed in any way recently?
✓ Has the employee been counselled about his performance before? Was this recorded?
✓ What is the employee's past history? Are there any current warnings?
✓ Are there any mitigating circumstances?
✓ Was it reasonable to expect such a performance from this person?
✓ Has the person had appropriate training and support, including the right materials and tools to do the job?
✓ Is the person suffering personal or medical problems?
✓ Does the case mark a departure from the person's normal standards of performance? If so, why?
✓ Have managers turned a blind eye to the employee's poor performance in the past?

✓ Have other employees performed equally poorly and not been disciplined?

✓ Consider current staffing levels. Could reduced staffing and increased pressure be having a negative impact on performance?

✓ Have there been changes within the organisation which could temporarily have an impact on performance?

✓ Are there any factors outside the organisation which may have a negative impact on the employee's performance?

✓ Consider relationships within the workplace; is there anything that could have a negative impact on the employee's work performance?

✓ Are there any indications that the employee is suffering from work-related stress which could be having a negative impact on his performance?

✓ Look at the following documents:
- 🖉 training record
- 🖉 induction checklist
- 🖉 employment contract/ terms/ offer letter
- 🖉 job description.

✓ Provided that your policy allows it, you can check CCTV and emails.

✓ Was any injury or damage caused by the poor work performance?

✓ What normally happens?

✓ Are the standards reasonable and clear? Have they been communicated to the workforce? Can you prove they were aware of the standard required?

✓ Has the employee got an up-to-date copy of the capability procedure?

✓ Are there any witnesses?

When you are taking a statement from a witness, consider the following questions:

✓ How close was the witness to the incident? It can be useful to ask the witness to draw a diagram.

✓ How clearly could the witness see what happened?

Appendix 4:
Checklist: informal advice

This is all about getting the employee's commitment to improve. It's only to be used where there's been a fairly minor breach of the standards. Only have one or two of this type of informal chat. If there's no improvement, move it to the formal stage.

Meet somewhere private and tell the employee that this is an informal conversation, that you will be taking some notes and will be happy to give a copy to the employee.

- ✓ Describe the standard of performance required by the company. Put this in specific and measurable terms, for example, 'The level of productivity required is fifty widgets per hour'.
- ✓ State what the employee's actual performance has been. You should be able to show there's a difference between the two. Provide the evidence that supports your view. Seek the employee's agreement that there is a problem with certain aspects of his performance. Ask the employee what he thinks the root cause of the problem is.
- ✓ Remind the employee that he is not being blamed for the problem and that you are on the employee's side.
- ✓ Ask the employee what he enjoys about the job. This may help to make the discussion easier and reduce any defensiveness on the employee's part.
- ✓ Consider any mitigating factors put forward, for example, problems in the employee's personal life.
- ✓ Restate what is expected in terms of job duties, outputs and targets. Avoid assuming that the employee knows everything that is expected of him.
- ✓ Ask the employee's opinion on what he can do to achieve improvement in performance.

✓ Discuss solutions and offer such help and support as you reasonably can to assist the employee in meeting standards. This may include making some adjustments to the work or providing some training.

✓ Seek to agree specific action points with the employee, the details of which will depend on whether or not any specific cause of unsatisfactory performance has been identified. Agree targets.

✓ Agree a timescale for the improvement to be achieved. It has to be reasonable – eight to ten weeks is probably more realistic than two weeks.

✓ Schedule a follow-up meeting to review the employee's performance and make sure that the meeting takes place.

✓ Advise of the consequences of the employee failing to meet standard i.e. move to the first stage of the formal disciplinary process.

✓ Make notes of the discussion. Give the employee a copy of the agreements.

Note: do not use the word 'warning' here. There are no informal warnings. We are aiming to advise the employee about the issue and guide him back to the required standard.

Appendix 5:
Sample letter: request to attend a formal disciplinary meeting

Mrs J Huggins
5 Parsnip Green
Shoreham-in-the-Wold
Herts

4th May [year]

<u>By post and by hand</u>

Dear Josie

Disciplinary Hearing, 7th May

Over the last few months, I have had several informal conversations with you about the rate at which you decorate cakes. During these conversations, which were documented, you agreed that your productivity rate is slower than that of your colleagues and that when you work on the cupcake line, it does mean that other members of staff have to slow down. Your productivity decorating individual cakes is also some 15% slower than the departmental average, although I do recognise that it is beautifully done. We have established that there are no reasons connected to your physical health, which are impacting upon your performance and you have received some additional training to help you work faster. I did suggest that you moved to the gingerbread products assembly line as there is less decoration and I felt you may be more easily able to keep up, but you said that you preferred not to. We reviewed progress last Friday and, although I recognise that there has been a little improvement, it is still well below that required. You should be able to process ten cupcakes a minute and decorate five individual cakes an hour. Details of the product sheets and rates of productivity are enclosed with this letter.

You are therefore requested to attend a formal meeting in our office on 7th May at 3pm to discuss these points. I will attend to present my concerns on behalf of the company. Andrea Simmonds, an independent HR advisor, will chair the meeting, and Cathy Jones will also attend to take notes.

If you would like to submit a written statement for consideration in advance of the hearing you may do so.

At the meeting you will be given the full opportunity to explain your case and answer the allegations. You may ask questions, dispute the evidence I have provided, provide your own evidence and otherwise argue your case. You may also put forward any mitigating factors which you consider relevant.

Because this is a formal meeting, you have the right to be accompanied at the meeting by either a work colleague (who has not been involved in the investigation) or an accredited union representative. Your companion may act as a witness, address the meeting and confer with you, but is not permitted to answer questions on your behalf.

I enclose a copy of our capability procedure.

No decision has yet been made, but I must inform you, if the disciplining officer finds that the case has been proved, the outcome of the meeting could result in a first warning.

You are reminded that you are under a duty to take all reasonable steps to attend this meeting.

If you would like access to documents or any other material to help you prepare yourself, please advise me so that I can ensure you have copies.

If you have any queries or concerns about any of the matters in this letter, please let me know and I will do my best to resolve the problem.

Yours sincerely

James Marshmallow
Manager

Enc:

Capability procedure
Production sheets – cupcakes
Production sheets – individual cakes
Notes from informal discussions
Training record

Appendix 6:
Sample letter: first warning

Mrs J Huggins
5 Parsnip Green
Shoreham-in-the-Wold
Herts

10th May [year]

<u>By post and by hand</u>

Dear Josie

First Warning

I write to confirm the points made to you at our formal meeting on 7th May. You were reminded of your right to be accompanied, but you chose to waive this right. I chaired the meeting. Cathy Jones was present as the note taker. The evidence was presented by James Marshmallow on behalf of the Company.

The hearing was held to discuss your poor work performance. The concerns raised by James are that although you can do the work on the cupcake line, it is very slow with the result that other members of staff have to slow down. The productivity sheets demonstrate that when you are not working on the cupcake line, the team produce between 400–500 additional cupcakes per hour. James also produced evidence that the time it takes you to decorate individual cakes is 15% slower than the departmental average.

When I explored this with you, you agreed that you were slower, though surprised that the difference in your rate of production and that of others is as substantial as it is. You feel that you are a perfectionist and want to do the work to the very best of your ability. You said that that you have a 100% record on the quality checks made on your work. I accept that this is true.

You have committed to James to try to work somewhat faster. James has agreed to give you further guidance to help you pace yourself.

You had the opportunity to see, and amend where appropriate, the notes that were taken in the meeting. You signed these to indicate they were a true representation of what had been discussed.

I listened carefully to your explanation and then adjourned to consider the facts and your representations. Now that I have had the opportunity to reflect fully upon the facts available to me, I have concluded that it is appropriate to issue a formal sanction on grounds of poor work performance.

This is a first stage warning and will remain live for six months. If you are able to increase your level of cake production to meet the production levels of your colleagues, and still maintain a level of quality which is acceptable to our QC people, the warning will be disregarded at the end of that time. However, if you are unable to increase the rate of your productivity, the Company will reserve the right to escalate the matter to the next stage of the formal disciplinary process.

You have the right to appeal against this warning. If you wish to do so, please write to Rob Sherbert within five days of receipt of this letter, stating the grounds for your appeal.

Please sign and return the attached copy of this warning. This will be placed on your personal file.

James has committed to support you as fully as possible to help you achieve the targets. If you feel you need any additional support, please ask James in the first instance and he will do what he reasonably can to assist.

Please let me know if you have any questions or concerns arising from this letter.

Yours sincerely

Andrea Simmonds
HR Advisor

Appendix 7:
The right to be accompanied

Employment Relations Act 1999

10. (1) This section applies where a worker–

(a) is required or invited by his employer to attend a disciplinary or grievance hearing, and

(b) reasonably requests to be accompanied at the hearing.

2) Where this section applies the employer must permit the worker to be accompanied at the hearing by a single companion who–

(a) is chosen by the worker and is within subsection (3),

(b) is to be permitted to address the hearing (but not to answer questions on behalf of the worker), and

(c) is to be permitted to confer with the worker during the hearing.

(3) A person is within this subsection if he is–

(a) employed by a trade union of which he is an official within the meaning of sections 1 and 119 of the Trade Union and Labour Relations (Consolidation) Act 1992,

(b) an official of a trade union (within that meaning) whom the union has reasonably certified in writing as having experience of, or as having received training in, acting as a worker's companion at disciplinary or grievance hearings, or

(c) another of the employer's workers.

Employment Relations Act 2004

37 Role of companion at disciplinary or grievance hearing

(2B) The employer must permit the worker's companion to–

(a) address the hearing in order to do any or all of the following–

> (i) put the worker's case;

> (ii) sum up that case;

> (iii) respond on the worker's behalf to any view expressed at the hearing;

(b) confer with the worker during the hearing.

(2C) Subsection (2B) does not require the employer to permit the worker's companion to–

(a) answer questions on behalf of the worker;

(b) address the hearing if the worker indicates at it that he does not wish his companion to do so; or

(c) use the powers conferred by that subsection in a way that prevents the employer from explaining his case or prevents any other person at the hearing from making his contribution to it.

Appendix 8:
Example of a PIP

To: J Huggins
From: J Marshmallow
Date: 2nd March

Subject: Performance Improvement plan (PIP)

1. This PIP has been developed between Josie Huggins and James Marshmallow, on 2nd March.

2. The purpose of this PIP is to provide you with an opportunity to raise your performance to the level required by specifying the key areas of unsatisfactory performance and a programme to meet these expectations. As a part of this you are offered the necessary support to give you every opportunity to achieve our agreed targets, as discussed in our meeting.

3. Your current performance is unsatisfactory in that you have failed to action agreed tasks within the required time. An example of this is the speed at which you are decorating cupcakes. The average production rate for the decoration of cupcakes is 10-12 per minute. You are working at the rate of an average of six–seven cupcakes per minute.

4. We discussed what can be done to help you. You have agreed to try to work at a faster rate. We have agreed that you will initially aim to complete an average of eight cupcakes per minute by 18th March. Thereafter, you should seek to increase your speed to nine cupcakes per minute by 4th April and ten cupcakes per minute by 16th April.

5. I will arrange some additional training to help you increase your speed and this will take place within the next two weeks. I have also suggested that you work on the gingerbread line as there is less

decoration and you are better able to keep up. You have indicated that you prefer to stay with the cupcakes; however, this remains an option. Please let me know if you wish to move to that line.

6. We will meet to review progress every two weeks. The first meeting will take place on 16th March. The purpose of this meeting is for you to be advised as to your progress towards reaching the objective. I will also take feedback from you, so that I can ensure that I am doing everything reasonably possible to support you.

7. If your performance does not meet the required standards, I am under a duty to advise you that I reserve the right to escalate the matter to the first stage of the formal disciplinary process.

Please let me know if you have any queries and I will do my best to resolve them.

_____

Manager's signature, and position title   Date

_____

Employee acknowledgement and declaration:

I acknowledge the terms of this PIP. I understand that if my performance remains unsatisfactory during the course of, and at the conclusion, of the PIP, disciplinary procedures may be undertaken.

_____

Employee's signature, and position title   Date

The HR Headmistress' Guide
How to Get Top Marks in ... Carrying Out Workplace Investigations

Kate Russell

If you enjoyed Kate's robust and practical style in *How to Get Top Marks in ... Managing Poor Work Performance,* then you will certainly be interested in her new book *How to Get Marks in ... Carrying Out Workplace Investigations.*

When workplace disputes arise, many managers shoot first and ask questions later (HR are always having to deal with the 'bodies'!) Needless to say, this is likely to seriously flaw the disciplinary process and put the final outcome in doubt. It is vitally important to collect and consider all the facts before taking any action.

The fundamental purpose of a discipline or grievance investigation is to collect the facts. It's no more difficult than that. But while a really rigorous investigation is essential to a well conducted process, many managers simply skate over the surface and either do not collect the relevant data or fail to take a sufficiently robust approach to data collection.

In The HR Headmistress' new book, the reader is guided through the process that employers should follow when conducting a formal workplace investigation. Readers will find out about the legal framework and learn how to identify and avoid the risks of unfair dismissal and unlawful discrimination claims during the investigation process. Kate takes her readers through the key skills needed to collect evidence and provides practical advice and exercises. This includes collecting data from witnesses, guidance on obtaining anonymous witness statements and the need to be objective and focus on facts. It's important to properly plan and prepare for the investigation and the book also includes guidance on what to do if difficulties arise. As well as guiding the reader though the fact-finding process, Kate considers how to manage stress and employee absence in the context of an investigation and the role of the investigator at a formal disciplinary or grievance meeting.

With its case studies, checklists and templates, *How to Get Top Marks in ... Carrying Out Workplace Investigations* is the essential handbook for any manager who is expected to carry out investigations.

Publication Date: 31st March 2011

RRP £5.00 (+P&P)

To pre-order your copy of *How to Get Top Marks in ... Carrying Out Workplace Investigations* call us on 0845 644 8955 or email: info@russellhrconsulting.co.uk

Index

Lightning Source UK Ltd.
Milton Keynes UK
18 September 2010

160019UK00002B/2/P